Santiago

Region of Araucania

Cautín River

Mount Llaima

Town of
Temuco
Cautin Province
1906

Punta Arenas

Lake District

Anyone who hasn't been in the Chilean forest doesn't know this planet.

I have come out of that landscape, that mud, that silence, to roam, to go singing through the world.

— Pablo Neruda

To Go Singing through the World

THE CHILDHOOD OF PABLO NERUDA

Deborah Kogan Ray

FRANCES FOSTER BOOKS
FARRAR, STRAUS AND GIROUX
NEW YORK

Pablo Neruda grew up in the Wild West of his country.

In the shadow of volcanoes and surrounded by giant rain forests, the mill town of Temuco was a tiny outpost in Araucania, on Chile's southern frontier.

The new railroad that crossed the Andes Mountains had opened the vast wilderness for settlement. It brought people from the cities and farm provinces of Chile, and from distant Europe and North America. They came to cut the ancient forests and labor in the dusty sawmills along the winding Cautín River, to homestead in the untamed hills and start businesses in town.

From axes and rain, it grew up,
that town of wood
recently carved, like
a new star stained with resin.

Temuco is a pioneer town, one of those towns that have no past. Since there was no common language among the settlers and many couldn't read, the shops hung eye-catching signs to announce their wares—*an enormous saw, a giant cooking pot, a Cyclopean padlock, a mammoth spoon. Farther along the street, shoe stores—a colossal boot.*

The boards of the house
smelled of the woods,
of the deep forest.

Our houses, then, had something of a settlers' temporary camp about them . . . Anyone who came in saw kegs, tools, saddles . . . There were always rooms that weren't finished, and half-completed stairways.
When winter came, storms blew up from the Antarctic. Winds howled like wolves and battered the poorly constructed houses. At times an eerie red glow that terrified Pablo appeared over the mountains. The earth would rumble. The house would shake. Mount Llaima, the volcano, was stirring.

Threads of rain fell, like long needles of glass snapping off on the roofs or coming up against the windows in transparent waves, and each house was a ship struggling to make port in the ocean of winter.

Hard, cold rain fell for months. The narrow, oxcart-rutted streets became seas of mud. Floods washed down the steep mountains and swept away the railroad tracks.

Pablo's father, Don José, was a railway man and chief of the repair crew. The boy worried when his father left on long runs into the mountains, and fretfully awaited his return.

> *My blunt father comes back*
> *from the trains.*
> *We recognize*
> *in the night*
> *the whistle*
> *of the locomotive*
> *perforating the rain*
> *with a wandering moan,*
> *lament of the night,*
> *and later*
> *the door shivering open.*

My mother, Doña Rosa Basoalto, died before I could have a memory of her . . . My father . . . married again; his second wife was Doña Trinidad Candia Marverde, my stepmother . . . the guardian angel of my childhood.

Doña Trinidad was descended from the native people of Araucania, the first Chileans, whom the settlers called Indians. Pablo called her "Mama," and loved her with all his heart.

When he awoke in the rain-haunted nights, Doña Trinidad told him stories of long ago, when her ancestors, the Mapuche, lived freely in the rain forest among the birds and animals under the giant rauli trees. The gentle rhythm of her whispered words sang to him.

Under the volcanoes, beside the snow-capped mountains, among the huge lakes, the fragrant, the silent, the tangled Chilean forest . . . The wild scent of the laurel, the dark scent of the boldo herb, enter my nostrils and flood my whole being.

After the long, hard winter, spring burst green and glorious in the rain forest; the perfume of jungle plants filled the air. To Pablo, the rain forest was an intoxicating place of discovery and wonder. He hunted for golden carabus beetles and red-haired spiders among quivering ferns that towered over him. He searched for minute insect treasures in the hollows of fallen trees and in the damp earth under rocks. He marveled at the perfection of blue partridge eggs hidden in dainty nests woven of moss and feathers.

A wild bird, with a voice like an oboe, called from high above in the tangled vines. Pablo answered.

He was never lonely in the rain forest. The music of earth sang to him.

I am alone
in the natal jungle,
in the deep
and black Araucania.
There are wings
which scissor at the silence,
a raindrop which falls
heavy and cold
like a horseshoe.
The forest sounds and is silent—
it is silent when I listen.
It sounds when I am asleep.

Pablo wanted to know what lay beyond the town and surrounding forest. His heart pounded with excitement when his father agreed to take him on the train run from Temuco to Carahue. The train roared across the countryside into the Araucanian wilderness, belching giant plumes of smoke.

It crossed immense, unpopulated, uncultivated terrain, crossed virgin forests, rumbled through tunnels and over bridges, like an earthquake.

It passed tribal villages with clusters of straw-roofed houses called *rucas*. The Mapuche had retreated to this corner of Araucania after three hundred years of fighting for the land they once roamed freely. It was hard for Pablo to believe that these gentle hills had been the scene of fierce battles between invading armies of Spanish conquistadors and the first Chileans.

Each station had a lovelier name, almost all of them inherited from the ancient Araucanian . . . These Araucanian names always signified something delicious: buried honey, lagoons or a river beside a forest, or a woodland with the name of a bird.

The words sang to Pablo when he rolled them on his tongue.

Families in traditional dress waited at the station stops to sell chickens, lambs, eggs, and boiled bread called *semita*. Blankets were spread with their handcrafts: intricately patterned textiles, heavy silver necklaces, and clay pots etched with the design of *cherruve*—the spirits of shooting stars.

To Pablo, the Mapuche people looked like the royalty from far-off kingdoms who were pictured on the covers of his books. He felt angry as he watched the passengers mill about the silent majestic families, rudely demanding bargains.

Pablo had saved all his pennies to buy a birthday present for Doña Trinidad. A rainbow-colored sash caught his eye, but he did not buy it. He was too shy to ask the price.

Pablo was intensely curious about everyone he met and fascinated by the world around him. He saw, heard, and felt everything acutely. He longed to speak the words that were inside him, but they would not come out. He was so afraid he would stutter in front of people, he pretended to have no interest in them and wore his silence like an overcoat.

Only gentle Doña Trinidad could coax words from Pablo, but, as was the custom of the time, she would turn into a shadow in his father's presence and become as mute as Pablo.

It's my father.
The centurions of the road surround him:
railwaymen wrapped in wet ponchos,
steam and rain cloaked the house
with them, the dining room was filled with
hoarse stories, glasses were drained.

I listened to the conversations at my father's table. But the next day, if I ran into those who had dined at my home the evening before, I didn't dare greet them, I even crossed over to the other side of the street to avoid embarrassment.

Shyness is a kink in the soul, a special category, a dimension that opens out into solitude.

On school days Pablo walked alone, past the mills piled with cut logs and mountains of sawdust, to a rambling old mansion that loomed high on a hill above the river. Once it had been the home of the provincial governor. Now it housed the school: girls on one side and boys on the other.

Pablo always felt like an outsider among the boisterous sons of the settlers. Even when invited, he rarely joined in their games.

Sometimes we would fight with acorns . . . Anyone who has never been hit by an acorn doesn't know how much it really hurts . . . I had little skill, no strength, and not much cunning. I always got the worst of it.

Classes were often a nightmare for Pablo. Though his compositions were excellent and he read very well, his tongue got stuck when the teacher called on him to recite, and his classmates snickered at his stutter. Their laughter stung him more than the acorns they threw.

He deliberately set himself apart and tried to be different.

I decided to wear a bright green rain hat. It belonged to my father, like the heavy woolen cape, the red and green signal lanterns, which I found so fascinating and took to school as soon as I got the chance, to strut around with them.

I would have dressed myself
in red roof tiles, in smoke,
to continue there, but invisible,
to attend everything, but at a distance,
to keep my own obscure identity
fastened to the rhythm of the spring.

Below his classroom window, the winding Cautín River
beckoned to Pablo. Much of his school day was spent dreaming
of escape.

Whenever he could, he would sneak away, run down the
hill to dip his feet in the cold rippling water. He didn't care if
he got punished. The river sang to him.

His father scolded him for his poor grades in mathematics. Before every test Pablo lived in dread of his father's tutorials. Don José ran the household in the same manner he managed his railroad repair crews. He directed all family activities with shrill blasts from his railwayman's whistle.

The boy knew that his father, who labored long hours for little pay, hoped that an education would give his son tools for a better life. But Pablo hated when Don José impatiently blew his whistle to speed his answers along.

And all the while I was moving in the world of knowing, on the turbulent river of books, like a solitary navigator.

I can't forget what I read last night: in faraway Malaysia, Sandokan and his friends survived on breadfruit. I don't like Buffalo Bill, because he kills Indians. But he's such a good cowpuncher!

Swashbuckling pirate stories by Emilio Salgari carried Pablo to exotic Asian seaports. He rode across the dusty plains of America's West with cowboys and Indians, and plied the Mississippi River with Huckleberry Finn.

Whenever he could escape, Pablo retreated to his river of books, his dreams of adventure, and the poems he wrote secretly.

I go upstairs to my room. I read Salgari. The rain pours down like a waterfall. In less than no time, night and the rain cover the whole world. I am alone, writing poems in my math notebook.

I really lived many of the first years of my life, and perhaps many of the next ones and the ones after that, as a kind of deaf mute.

I didn't want to be seen,
I didn't want my existence to be known.
I became pallid, thin, and absentminded.
I didn't want to speak so that nobody
would recognize my voice, I didn't want
to see so that nobody would see me.
Walking, I pressed myself against the wall
like a shadow slipping away.

Pablo lived in a world unknown to his strict father or gentle stepmother—a world where words and images burned in his mind.

I wander off into the countryside and I walk, walk, walk. I become lost on Ñielol Hill. I am alone, my pocket filled with beetles. In a box I carry a hairy spider I just caught. Overhead, the sky can't be seen . . . A chill of warning creeps upward from my feet.

Pablo was as protected in his shell as the beetles he collected, as elusive as the spider spinning out of reach on unseen silken thread.

Like Mount Llaima, he was a silent, waiting volcano; fires were stirring deep within him.

As Pablo was growing, so was the town of Temuco. More people arrived and new houses were built. A small public library opened and a newspaper was published each week that announced local events.

Pablo was asked to report on school events. He enjoyed every moment of the assignment and wrote vivid descriptions of soccer games and school celebrations, but he never signed his stories. He wanted to avoid conflict with his father, who would be displeased to know that he neglected his studies to write for the newspaper.

Around this time, a tall lady who wore long long dresses and flat shoes came to Temuco.

Pablo was entering his final year of school when a new principal for the girls' division arrived from Chile's southernmost city, Punta Arenas. Like Doña Trinidad, she was descended from the first Chileans.

Her name was Gabriela Mistral, and she was a poet. She had been awarded a national prize for her book of verse, *Sonnets of Death*.

To be a woman author was a rarity in those days in Chile. Though few of the townspeople had read her book, and the small public library had no copy, the celebrated new principal was the subject of much gossip and speculation in Temuco.

To Pablo, she was a deep mystery.

I used to watch her passing through the streets of my home town, with her sweeping dresses, and I was scared of her.

He was terrified when he was summoned to Gabriela Mistral's office.

Gabriela Mistral had invited Pablo because she had seen his newspaper articles. She was impressed by his fine use of language and wanted to meet the student reporter.

In her dark face, as Indian as a lovely Araucanian pitcher, her very white teeth flashed in a full, generous smile that lit up the room.

But solemn Pablo barely heard her compliments about his writing or her gentle inquiries about his interests. Overcome by timidity, he didn't say a word. In a desperate effort to avoid eye contact, he stared at the bookshelves in her office. He had never seen so many books belonging to one person.

Seeing the boy's discomfort and his attention to her books, she invited him to select one and suggested a new translation of a long Russian novel, *War and Peace* by Leo Tolstoy, that was her favorite.

Gabriela Mistral opened new worlds to Pablo.

He returned to borrow more Russian novels, and soon read everything by Tolstoy, Dostoevsky, and Chekhov that she owned. She introduced him to French stories, Italian poetry, English plays, and the writings of Greek philosophers.

My appetite for reading did not let up day or night . . . I gobbled up everything.

He awoke each morning anticipating the late afternoon, when he would engage in long discussions of world literature with Señorita Gabriela. She was always interested in hearing his ideas and opinions, and did not seem to notice if he stuttered.

Pablo's protective shell began to crack and slowly open.

One afternoon, with great trepidation, he asked if he could borrow her prizewinning book. That night he read for the first time her graceful poetry. The words that came from Gabriela's heart sang to Pablo. He knew that he could trust her.

The next day, Pablo arrived with his notebooks and opened up his secret world to her.

Once, far back in my childhood, when I had barely learned to read, I felt an intense emotion and set down a few words, half rhymed but strange to me, different from everyday language.

Gabriela read the notebooks over and over. As a teacher, she was amazed by the phrasing, the descriptive language, and the maturity of the writing. As a poet, she heard Pablo's solitary call and recognized in the isolated boy the hidden voice of another poet.

Gabriela urged Pablo to write all the words that were in his heart: to sing his songs and allow the world to hear them.

With her encouragement and constant friendship, Pablo threw himself into writing.

He wrote of the terrible rain-swept winters and of the wonder-filled rain forest. He wrote about his life in Temuco, and of the glorious wild country of Araucania and its native people. He wrote about his fears and loneliness, and he wrote about the people that he loved. His words burned like fire, spilled from the pages like molten lava. They sang and soared.

Poetry gave Pablo his voice.

Gabriela helped Pablo obtain a scholarship to study at the university in Santiago, Chile's capital. When he was sixteen years old, he said goodbye to the world he knew in Temuco to begin his new life as a poet.

I grew up in this town, my poetry was born between the hill and the river, it took its voice from the rain, and like the timber, it steeped itself in the forests.

And that sharp chirp of the cricket
raising its plaint
in the unyielding solitude turns into
my song, my own song.

Pablo took with him the songs of his childhood in the rain forest, to go singing through the world.

Poetry

And it was at that age . . . poetry arrived
in search of me. I don't know, I don't
   know where
it came from, from winter or a river.
I don't know how or when,
no, they were not voices, they were not
words, not silence,
but from a street it called me,
from the branches of night,
abruptly from the others,
among raging fires
or returning alone,
there it was without a face,
and it touched me.

I didn't know what to say, my mouth
had no way
with names,
my eyes were blind.
Something knocked in my soul,
fever or forgotten wings,
and I made my own way,
deciphering
that fire,
and I wrote the first, faint line,
faint, without substance, pure
nonsense,
pure wisdom

of someone who knows nothing;
and suddenly I saw
the heavens
unfastened
and open,
planets,
palpitating plantations,
the darkness perforated,
riddled
with arrows, fire and flowers,
the overpowering night, the universe.

And I, tiny being,
drunk with the great starry
void,
likeness, image of
mystery,
felt myself a pure part
of the abyss.
I wheeled with the stars.
My heart broke loose with the wind.

La poesía

Y fue a esa edad . . . Llegó la poesía
a buscarme. No sé, no sé de dónde
salió, de invierno o río.
No sé cómo ni cuándo,
no, no eran voces, no eran
palabras, ni silencio,
pero desde una calle me llamaba,
desde las ramas de la noche,
de pronto entre los otros,
entre fuegos violentos
o regresando solo,
allí estaba sin rostro
y me tocaba.

Yo no sabía qué decir, mi boca
no sabía
nombrar,
mis ojos eran ciegos,
y algo golpeaba en mi alma,
fiebre o alas perdidas,
y me fui haciendo solo,
descifrando
aquella quemadura,
y escribí la primera línea vaga,
vaga, sin cuerpo, pura
tontería,
pura sabiduría

del que no sabe nada,
y vi de pronto
el cielo
desgranado
y abierto,
planetas,
plantaciones palpitantes,
la sombra perforada,
acribillada
por flechas, fuego y flores,
la noche arrolladora, el universo.

Y yo, mínimo ser,
ebrio del gran vacío
constelado,
a semejanza, a imagen
del misterio,
me sentí parte pura
del abismo,
rodé con las estrellas,
mi corazón se desató en el viento.

Author's Note

The great Latin American writer Gabriel García Márquez called Pablo Neruda "the greatest poet of the twentieth century—in any language."

Along with my narrative, I have used Pablo Neruda's own words, translated from the Spanish language, to tell his story. His life was made up of many facets, and he shared of himself in both poems and prose. I have used segments from his prose account *Memoirs*—primarily from the chapter "The Country Boy," which details his early childhood.

I have also incorporated lines from a poem in *Canto General* and lines from several poems in Neruda's verse autobiography, *Memorial de Isla Negra*. "Poetry," included in English translation and its original Spanish ("La poesía"), is from that collection.

Pablo Neruda (1904–1973)

Pablo Neruda was born Neftalí Ricardo Reyes Basoalto in Parral, in Chile's fertile central valley. His mother died of tuberculosis when he was one month old, and he lived with his grandparents for his first two years. When his father remarried, he brought the boy to the frontier town of Temuco.

Pablo Neruda is the pen name, later changed legally, that he adopted when he began to publish poems. A recognized poet by the time he was twenty, Pablo Neruda became Latin America's most celebrated literary figure. During his long career, he wrote thousands of poems. He wrote about the rain forest where he lived as child, and about the faraway places where he roamed. A master of language, he wrote about pain and love, people and history, and his hope for a better world. In 1971, he was awarded the Nobel Prize in Literature "for a poetry that with the action of an elemental force brings alive a continent's destiny and dreams."

Neruda was not only a great poet but also an ardent political activist who used his celebrity to call attention to social injustice. He served his country as a diplomat in the Far East and in Europe, and was elected by the farmers and miners of the impoverished mountain area of Tarapacá to represent them in the Chilean Senate.

Often referred to as the "people's poet," Neruda believed that a "poet's obligation" was to become a voice for all those who had no voice.

Gabriela Mistral (1889–1957)

Gabriela Mistral was already a nationally recognized poet when she arrived in Temuco and met young Pablo Neruda. She would later become a pioneering educator in Mexico, a cultural ambassador in Europe, Chile's representative to the United Nations, and a great spokesperson for the world's children. In 1945, she became the first Latin American woman to win the Nobel Prize in Literature.

Gabriela Mistral and Pablo Neruda remained friends until her death in 1957.

Chronology of Pablo Neruda

1904   Born on July 12 in Parral, Chile.

1906   Moves to Temuco.

1910–20 Attends Temuco's school for boys. Meets Gabriela Mistral.

1921–23 Studies at the University of Chile in Santiago. Contributes poems and articles to *Claridad*, a magazine published by the Student Federation of Chile.

1924   Publishes *Veinte poemas de amor y una canción desesperada* (Twenty Love Poems and a Song of Despair). It receives national acclaim.

1927–32 Appointed to diplomatic posts in Burma, Ceylon, Java, and Singapore. Writes of his experiences, decrying the social conditions in Southeast Asia.

1935   Appointed to consular position in Spain. Neruda becomes a close friend of poet Federico García Lorca. They publish a newspaper that supports the Spanish Republic.

1936–37 Spanish Civil War breaks out. García Lorca is murdered by the opposing Fascists. Neruda assumes the role of advocate for the Republic, despite Chilean government orders that he must be politically neutral. He resigns his post and aids Spanish refugees fleeing to France.

1938–40 Travels in Latin America speaking against fascism. Appointed consul for emigration of Spanish refugees in Paris. World War II spreads throughout Europe.

1941–44 Serves as consul general to Mexico. Writes

poems for *Canto general*, a history of the South American continent.

1945–47 Impoverished miners and farmers elect Neruda to the national Senate. World War II ends. Neruda joins the Communist Party. Chilean government imposes censorship of the press.

1948–49 Neruda delivers Senate speech accusing government of betraying Chilean working people. The government orders his arrest. He escapes over the Andes Mountains.

1950–52 Lives in exile in Europe until his arrest order is revoked. He returns to Chile in August 1952, where he is greeted as a national hero.

1953–64 His reputation grows worldwide. *Memorial de Isla Negra* is published to celebrate his sixtieth birthday.

1970 He is nominated to run for the presidency of Chile, but steps aside to support his friend Salvador Allende, who is elected.

1971 Neruda is awarded the Nobel Prize in Literature.

1973 Chile's elected government is overthrown by a military coup. Allende is killed. Neruda's house is ransacked and he is declared an enemy. He dies of cancer on September 23 in Santiago. Though threatened with imprisonment, thousands of Chileans attend the funeral of the "people's poet."

Acknowledgments

My thanks to the Fundación Pablo Neruda and the Carmen Balcells Literary Agency in Barcelona, and to the following for permission to use portions of Pablo Neruda's poems and memoirs in the making of this book:

Canto General Fiftieth Anniversary Edition, translated/edited by Jack Schmitt, six lines from Schmitt's translation of the poem titled "The House." Copyright © 1991 by Fundación Pablo Neruda and the Regents of the University of California Press. Used by permission of the publisher.

Excerpts from "The Journey," "The Father," "The South," "Shyness," and "Poetry" from *Isla Negra* by Pablo Neruda, translated by Alastair Reid. Translation copyright © 1981 by Alastair Reid. Reprinted by permission of Farrar, Straus and Giroux, LLC.

Excerpts from "The Country Boy," "Lost in the City," and "My Country in Darkness" from *Memoirs* by Pablo Neruda, translated by Hardie St. Martin. Translation copyright © 1976, 1977 by Farrar, Straus and Giroux, LLC. Reprinted by permission of Farrar, Straus and Giroux, LLC.

And my gratitude to Francisco Picado for translating additional research material.

For Karen and Francisco

Distributed in Canada by Douglas & McIntyre Ltd.
Color separations by Chroma Graphics PTE Ltd.
Printed and bound in China by South China Printing Co. Ltd.
Designed by Barbara Grzeslo
First edition, 2006
1 3 5 7 9 10 8 6 4 2

www.fsgkidsbooks.com

Library of Congress Cataloging-in-Publication Data
Ray, Deborah Kogan, date.
  To go singing through the world : the childhood of Pablo Neruda / Deborah Kogan Ray.— 1st ed.
    p. cm.
  ISBN-13: 978-0-374-37627-7
  ISBN-10: 0-374-37627-1
  1. Neruda, Pablo, 1904–1973—Childhood and youth—Juvenile literature. 2. Poets, Chilean—20th century—Biography—Juvenile literature. I. Title.

PQ8097.N4 Z7255 2006
861/.62 B—dc22

2005044317

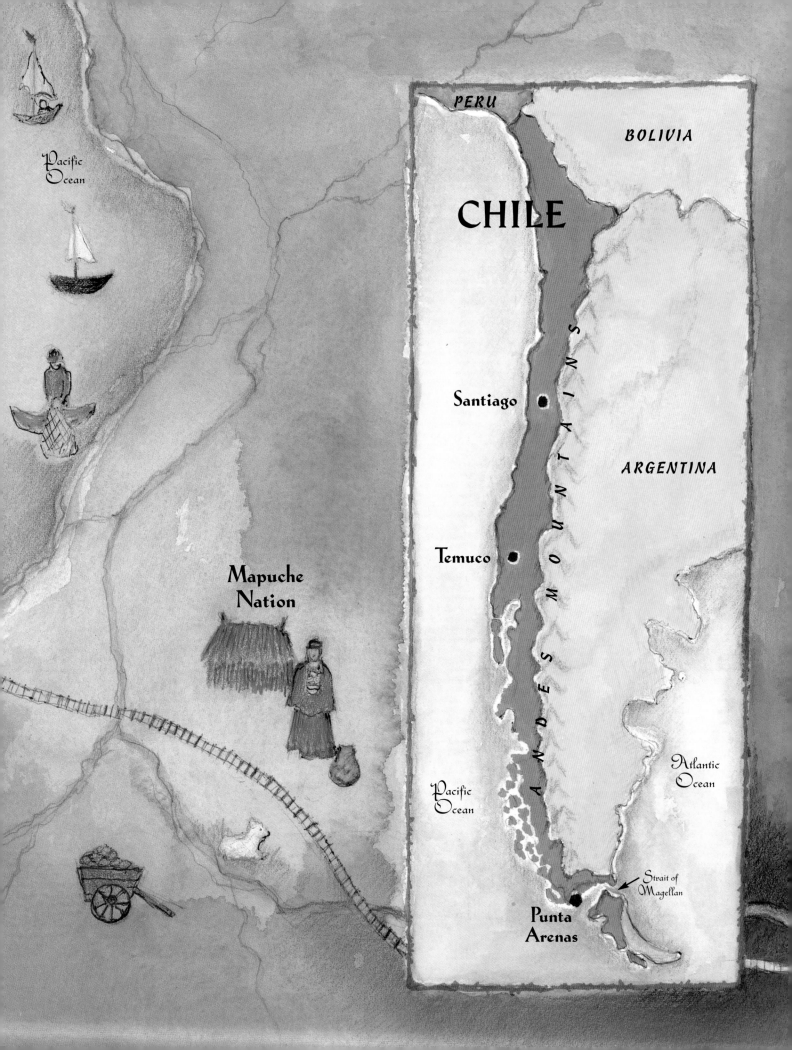